Post-its from my Grey Matter

Tangled verses

Ilisha Bhagwat

BookLeaf Publishing

India | USA | UK

Cover design inspiration: Akancha Singh
Made with ❤ on the BookLeaf Publishing Platform
www.bookleafpub.in
www.bookleafpub.com

Dedication

To everyone who has ever evoked an emotion
in me, triggering the desire to knit those
words into a beautiful poem.

Acknowledgement

To me, writing was an escape, and my Notepad was a savior. Thank you for not just being an app on my phone, but my favorite confidant.

The two pillars in my life who played a pivotal role: Dear Kanchu, thank you for being the one to 'gift' me a beautiful visualization of how my book would look like. And, Somu, I cannot thank you enough for being my strongest support in this journey.

My dog Rubik, my parents, Prasham, Adu and family for loving me unconditionally and believing in me.

Lastly, my support, my friends and colleagues, who passionately read my writing and have been a constant encouragement.

Here's to an inward glance at my world.

Preface

"Feel an itch? Just write it out"

Silence is often associated with the inability to convey emotions. However, for some people, emotions might reflect on a piece of paper. Written words also have the power to heal and engage with the deepest, most complex algorithms of feelings embodied within us.

In a room full of people, I have always been a silent observer. If you catch me staring at a random pillow, I'm most probably making notes in my mind. Expressing a surge of happiness, sadness or strong opinions verbally has always been a difficult task for me. A fight, an argument, a feeling of sudden joy, accomplishments, pride, rejection and heartbreak would often end up in the notepad of my phone at the end of the day. This notepad is my diary and dearest friend.

When I felt the slightest itch, I just wrote it out.

This book is basically a sneak peek into my imagination of how 'that' one conversation might have gone if only I had let my words leave my mouth.

These are post-its from my memory, my grey matter.

Index

An Ode from Psyche

It's a working Wednesday,
My fingertips are dancing to laptop keys,
Eyes measuring the Excel sheets,
Vocal cords humming to meetings.
My physical body is an absolute robot,
Not reacting but responding to a stimulus
And contradicting Aristotle's concept of a
body and soul.
What is a body without soul?
Just flesh and blood,
And maybe bones.
In this moment, my body and soul are not
one.
They live in different dimensions.
My body pretending to be a workaholic,
And my soul acting like a drunkard,

Drowning in a sea of thoughts.
With the passing hours and phased
withdrawals,
I slowly diverge from reality.
Only wishing that my imagination was
documented,
I hastily pick up my notepad,
And scribble a rhyme with musicality.

Melody

I sing lullabies of your deeds –
Country, Jazz, and Oldies.
Prelude of your love –
Mornings with symphony and
Other days of melancholy.
You hit the Ode of Joy,
Very classic,
Irrepressible.
My heart beats to your strings.
They never go offbeat because of the
fine-tuning you bring.
I wish I were your Carol.
Your hymn in the shower.
Your melody on dark days,
And a chant of enlightenment.

With the love you offer-
You are the Beethoven to my dead flower.
YOU are the greatest soul song,
Unforgettable,
For all of my seven lives to devour.

My Reflection saved me

Half past nine and it strikes my mind,
I am still turning the pages of a book,
And playing songs on rewind.
I live like a hopeless wanderer,
With no name to my life.
I wish I could give it a meaning,
Like Paolini titled *Saphira*.
My right eye blinks like a bad omen,
As I stare at the fairy lights on the wall.
My smile fades as dreams, slowly slip away,
One by one till I am left with none.
Tears crawl down the curve of my cheeks,
I can taste the salt of an endless sea.
Alas, the staircase is so long to measure
And I am not even halfway there.

On my left, you are living a perfect life
But my right says otherwise.
I look up and the sky is covered in velvet,
But my crushed ambitions wished for yellow
chimes.
My reflection spoke to me and said,
*'You better drag yourself to the stairs or the
shyness will eat you alive'*
It told me not to lie around like a book
covered in dust.
And made me believe that the words buried
beneath my armor,
Will bloom into a beautiful story.

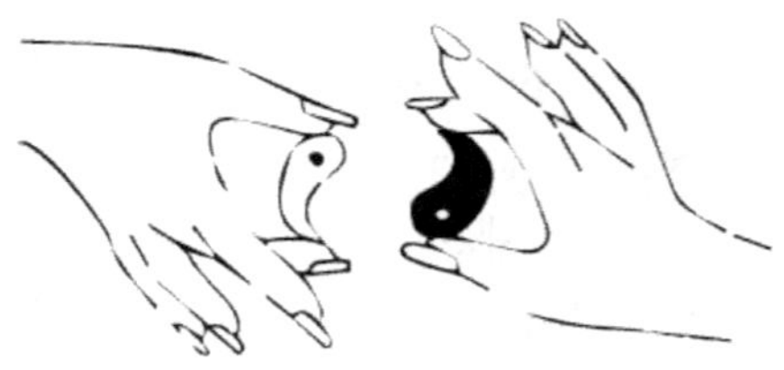

Black and White

Two outfits.
One black and one white,
Like angels and demons written in Da Vinci
code,
Reside in me to unleash themselves against
life's triggers.
When I met you, the war came to an end,
And my heart raised a peace treaty.
Your mother used to tell you that I am an
angel in disguise,
While you saw the demon in bed.
You have also seen me jolly,
When you held the door for me
And you said I had a sinful smile.
Oh, you were such a delight to have.
Your kindness was all I craved,

But sadly, you took it to the grave.
It's been seven years today and now I've
decided to go on a date.
So, tell me, what should I wear, love?
Pick an outfit for me,
Is it black today or white?

Colorless

Oh! That is a pretty skirt and a cool pair of
jeans,
A bold red dress,
Very effortless to keep.
My confidence comes in intervals
And mutism stays at its peak
My brain cells fail to function
And a pimple pops in heat.
I look at your red dress
And it screams Halloween to me.
But when I see you clad in it,
That screams perfect to me.
I am dumbfounded by the energy you carry
within.
My art to live is not even an atom of it.

How gracefully you walk down an aisle,
It's like you are getting married.
All eyes in the room are on you,
Two of which are mine.
I envy your existence, grace and courage—
Because what you see is 'Red'.
And that seems nothing,
But 'Grey' to me.

You

I want you.
I want to share *my* everything with you.
My every *day*, every *hour*, my every *minute*.
I want you to be the warmth on a cold
gloomy day.
I want you to be the reason my seventeen
muscles pull up just to form that beautiful
smile.
I want you to be the rainbow that fills colors
in my black-and-white pictures.
I want you to embolden me with words, so
that I grow, and we grow –
Just like those heavenly flowers that blossom
in the radiant sun.

Just like those tiny thin threads which
artistically entangle to form an elegant
wedding gown.
I want to build a house with you, right from
scratch.
I want that old-school love.
I want a healthy love, one that's a delight and
not a nightmare I dread.
I want that.
I want *us*.
I want *you*.

Love: One by two

I don't know what half-love is,
Or what is half of love –
Because mine is a river stream which keeps
running in bars.
It tastes like bitter alcohol,
And I drown in it.
I take you with me, from crossroads to
eternity.
We feel it all and we feel it within.
You spot your reflection in between lines,
Sometimes in a poem and sometimes when I
drink wine.
When I touch you, it's wholesome.
Perfection to a point that I see my universe in
it.
When my heart speaks of you,

anger, animosity and hurt forget their
meaning.
Your happiness is a pill I would want to
overdose with,
And my love is the most invaluable gift you
would ever receive.
This emotion might drain me and make me
sick,
But I can assure you, that this love is electric
and complete.
Please engrave this on the piece of my heart:
I don't know what half-love is.
I don't know what it means to care in half.
I don't know what the other half is,
And I hope I never get a chance to.

Adrenaline

Your presence is my solid rock and my
endorphin high.
It is the first glimpse of morning sunshine,
The peace to my stormy seas
And a cosy nest to my restless mind.
Your touch is enchanting as it traces the
broken coastline of my body.
Just the sight of you is a dose of adrenaline to
kick-start my day.
On the gloomy winter days when you glance
at me,
I feel the warmth of the sun.
Your words are music to my ears,

While my heart strings to your tunes.
Your smile is a love language I never wish to
unlearn.
Your eyes, your body and just you,
are glowing sapphires,
which are to be cherished till eternity.

Loneliness

It's been days since my lips have been glued
because I have not spoken a word.
The gulp in my throat has grown heavier,
Because the air won't leave my lungs.
I want to scream at the top of my voice,
But I am too scared of being perceived as a
maniac.
It's a euphoric experience to scream with
someone,
And talk about your deepest interests, day
and night,
Till your oesophagus turns dry.
All these imaginations just make me smile,
because loneliness can eat you alive.
I start my day alone, and go to bed alone with
no words uttered.

Loneliness is a demon whose virtue is to
slowly poison your brain.
It feeds on your killed desires, your fading
confidence, deafening silence—
And finally, you.

Save the Children

The ceiling above stares back at me,
and I look at a blank slate which is covered in
white.
I wonder what splash of color I would throw,
to satisfy my evil mind?
This cruel world fathoms nothing simple,
Just frequent crimes to earn a dime.
The man is turning diabolical,
hatred is spreading like mushrooms,
our hearts are weary of kindness,
only fearing the act of terror.
I wish there were no counter colors,
only grey for being indecisive.
It is exhausting to live in a world like this-
Where wrong overpowers the right.

I wish there was a neutral.
A world where people have opinions and not
beliefs.
This apprehension of a terrible future,
makes me cold and lifeless.
This future belongs to our children.
And I want nothing, but peace for them.

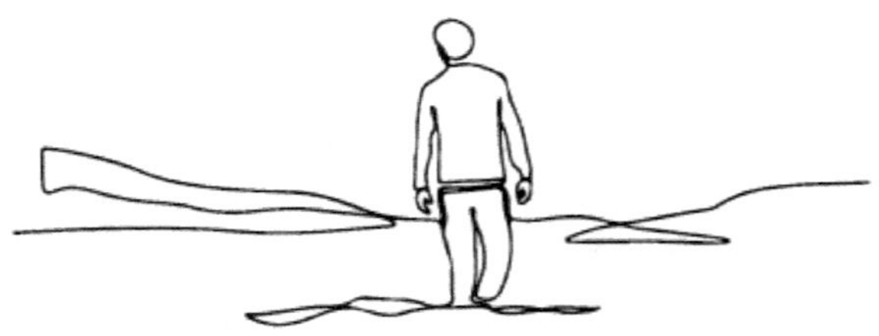

Gem

My thoughts are wired, and they prick my
nerves.
My grey matter is a dump yard of unnecessary
waste.
It mints tons of methane because I wish my
assumptions would get burnt in hell,
and my black heart turns soft again.
You set a foot on my land,
and radiate this divine positivity.
You turned my stones to jewels.
I called you a gem, the first time I met you.
I still mean it now, because you make me
shine,
Shinier than ever.

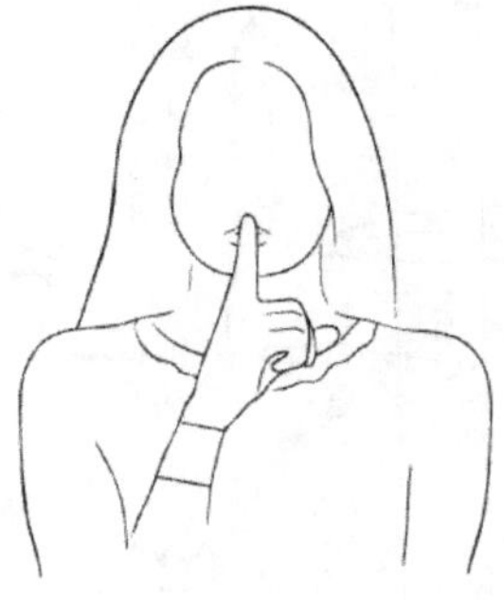

Fifth sense

One fine day I opened my eyes for the first
time on Earth.
It was the day I was born.
By God's grace, I had all five senses—
Eyes to see.
Ears to hear.
Skin to feel.
And tongue to well, speak.
Yet I sit across the table,
Uncomfortably mute.
I am that side of bacon,
Everyone chooses to ignore.
I hate not being seen, because I am left
unheard.

I presume, I am easy to forget.
My silence is so common.
Pity, even that is not loud enough.

Pause

I never believed in destiny,
Or in a strong force of attraction which
claims to be a power law—
Which makes your wishes come true.
I never knew what 'soul searching', 'gut
feeling' and the 'inner voice' meant until
yesterday.
It's true, the universe speaks to you.
It gleams of signals every now and then,
But only the blessed ones seem to notice.
Pause, before you make a decision.
Think, before you say something out loud.
Close your eyes, when your thoughts are
running a thousand miles an hour.
Breathe, when you are in a Gordian knot.

That moment of respite can change your perceptions, your decisions.
And your mind keeps its calm amidst all the terrible chaos.

The Gut Feeling

It's been a long season of blues.
My fingertips don't dance to alphabets
anymore.
I have a constant frown on my face, as I stare
at the flashing screen of sorrows.
My emotions are glued, and I feel everything
at once.
'Gut-wrenching' is a strong situation.
The churn inside me speaks of the devil.
Should I listen to him? Summon to him?
Or should I fight with him and travel to the
other side?

This feeling is the first ache of the dawn and
the last tear of the dusk.
It shrinks my body day by day and hour by
hour.
Oh lord, devour me with some hacks to this
mind-draining puzzle, because I am a lost
cause.
This gut feeling kills my hunger, my affection.
Just end it, so I can die in peace.

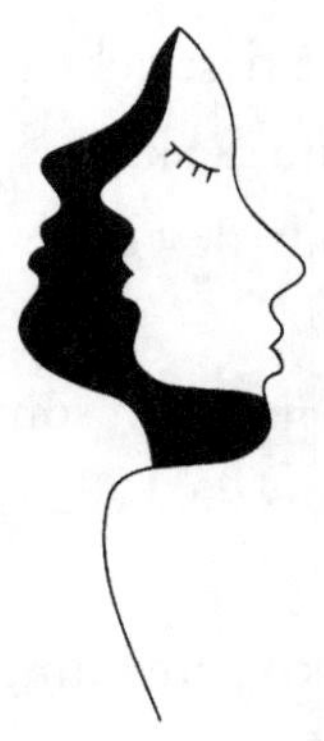

He

He.
He called me and said,
not how I was so pretty, but how I was so hot.
He called me and said,
not how I was so smart, but how my waist
seemed so slim.
He called and asked,
not what I was doing, but what I was wearing.
He called me and asked,
not about the size of my brain but about the
size of my bra.
He called me and asked,
not how I could understand him, but how I
could satisfy him.

Lastly,
He called me and said,
how attractive I was that he never even
fancied another woman.
That day I realized the difference between a
Man and a Hu-Man.
Where one, fantasizes a body.
The other, loves a soul.

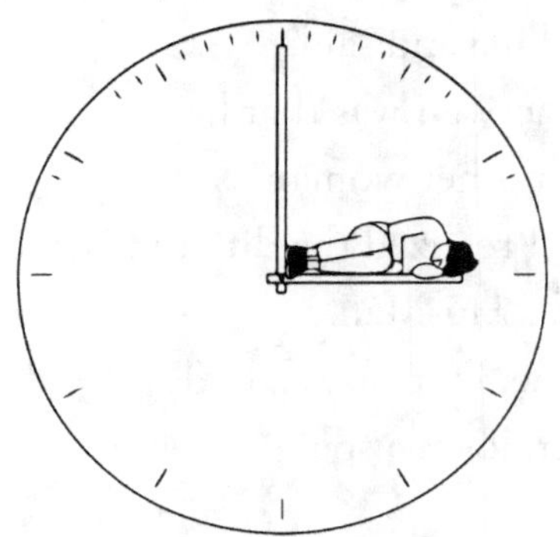

Counting Days

Day one, two, three,
We met and we talked.
You smiled, and I felt carefree.
Day four, five, six,
We clicked and we touched,
And you gave my heart a fix.
Day seven, eight, nine,
We spent the night together,
And poured our hearts over wine.
Day ten, eleven, twelve,
You met my mom, and we went on a date.
We booked a room and made love on the
shelves.

Day thirteen, fourteen, fifteen,
I was in love with you.
But when I turned around, I couldn't find you
next to me in bed.
Day sixteen, seventeen and eighteen,
You stole my surrendered love, my heart and
my body.
I was left hollow and empty from within,
Having nothing to offer, because you took
them with you, and,
You never came back.

Intoxicated home

In our little 'home' called love,
Which is the cushion of comfort we return to.
It might not always be colourful, as there are
days it might look grey too.
My ear echoes of the exhausting days of
patience,
After the fight we had.
Those quiet, silent moments,
Overpowering the words and feelings we
always meant.
That slight pause we take,
Just to restrict ourselves and our will to speak
with each other.

The dawn arrives, and at 6 PM,
We hug like we cannot let go.
The next hour I brush my fingers through
your hair.
You close your eyes,
And I revere your irresistible smile.
We sync in kisses,
And our hands are glued.
With no words uttered,
We sink in the ocean of colourful hues.
We exchange letters of apologies,
And a series of unwavering efforts.
Mutually we wish to time travel,
And never undo this cyclical process,
Of pure, intoxicated, home-ly addiction.

Sunsets - You

It was a pleasant winter evening of
November,
When the clock ticked 6 PM,
And the dawning sun turned the sky yellow.
The breeze brushed my cheeks,
As I sat alone on the balcony.
I looked at birds chirping and flying away,
Back to their nests.
The sun gradually set,
And I started to hit my low, as I always do.
My mind started making these romantic
scenarios,
Wondering,
What if you and I were together, right now?
Me in your arms,

Cuddling and watching the sun meeting its
beloved on the other side of the earth.
Maybe, we sip a glass of smoothie I prepared
and,
Listen to our favorite song together.
You, kiss me on my forehead.
While I, curl up in your arms like a prawn.
It feels so innocent, so safe. So secure.
Slowly, I watch you fade away.
I have a love-hate feeling for evenings.
Love, because you visit my head, and I smile.
Hate- because my heart feels heavy watching
you fade as the sun sets.

Too good to be true

I drown in hurt,
As you chant the name.
I am shy, yet kind,
Showing love in frames.
I bleed in tears,
And die a little,
While you reminisce the moments,
Of past affairs.
I wish you loved me,
For what I had to offer,
For what I looked like,
Because I cannot wait any longer.
My shadow follows me, to the dungeon of
sorrow,

You love me, you love me not?
I sit on the fence juggling answers I forcefully
swallow.
I believe you lived a life too good to be true,
And I know I am not,
Half of what you already had.

JuJu

I love you,
Like it's Juju.
It's enchanting, yet tricky.
It acts like a magic with a poison,
And my heart is in the potion.
Your love is a spell and my mind is bewitched.
I am dizzy but I am also dreamy.
I feel loved but I also feel lost.
My life bleeds neutral,
Pale undertones and basic.
Even my smile was reserved,
The curve never reached my cheeks.
But, after your witchcraft,

It slides to my ears, as smooth as silk.
You are irresistible,
And this love is mystic.
Spellcasts are good and bad.
But I hope, this one,
Is not fatal.

Whisper

I saw you talking one fine day,
and your lips hardly sailed.
The air was thin, my gaze was sharp,
and heart sank a hundred thousand feet deep.
All I could hear were troubled whispers.
A true cacophony to me.
What was so intimate?
Your palms wrapped around the cheeks,
Is it dug so deep?
That feeling you are hiding from me.
I fail to understand how rhythm works,
wondering if our hearts are in sync?
'Welcome to my humble abode' and I let your
energy in.

Are we the missing pieces of a puzzle?
or are you still finding the perfect fit?
You look rather happy with me,
but is it the happiest you have ever been?
Love is deep-rooted and grows stronger with
time, they say.
How do you feel today, compared to the first
day we met?
It is almost Christmas, cuddly and cold.
Tell me, love,
Will you still be here at home?

Tears

Yellow light, too bright.
Scrolling through others' ambitions,
My eyes seem to pry.
My vision is caged,
Just to realize it's too late.
Because I got no tears left to cry.

Knitted sunsets

How do you feel?
Reliving those beautiful moments
Again, in time.
Spending netted hours together,
in the same bed you two fell in love?
How do you feel, being one again?
it was supposed to be us,
the ones who come back home
Together,
after seeing the world.
How does it feel, to be living the life your
younger self yearned for?
because I am still frozen in 2021,
Spending netted hours alone,
watching the same sunset,
the one where I fell in love with you.

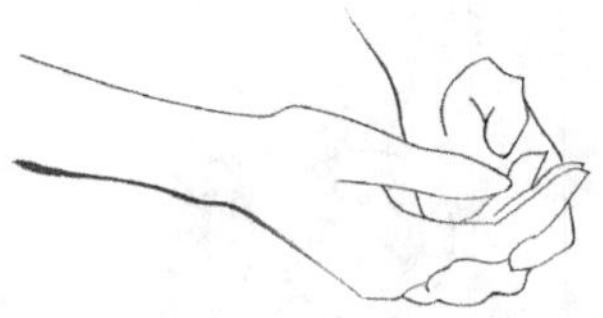

Questions

What do you see in me?
Is my most frequently asked question.
Is it my presence that comforts your anxious
mind?
Or my hug that feels like a glove of warmth?
Do I seem important to you?
Or am I as good as a conjunction, helping
your wounds come together?
Do you picture us together?
In all smiles and teary eyes of happiness?
Is all this just a fairy tale to me?
My imaginations are cocaine-high
while you are just sober and neutral?
Tell me,
What do you see in me?
So, I can blissfully smile
Or be dumb for life.

Awkward

How does it feel?
To be nature's favorite?
Everything comes to you with ease.
Conversations are an exam to me,
Which I fail,
Because I drown in anxiety.
I am shy.
I am quiet.
I am socially awkward.
And I don't want to be reminded,
Again,
And
Again.
Social engagements are triggers.
My mind is under constant pressure.

I lose my sanity,
While words look jumbled to me.
I don't want to be reminded,
Again,
And
Again,
That I am nothing,
But boring.

One, two, three

I woke up to a phone call,
And disturbed sleep,
Next to the beach, I decided to take a walk.
The water was cold,
My feet almost frozen
I started picking shells
One, two, three,
Hurt.
I named each one,
Words.
Mistakes.
Pain
And, *trigger.*
I decided to never walk alone by the sea,
And,
Pick pieces of the past,
Which are never washed away.

Tied by thread

I am walking on a thread
I bend and I fall,
So deep, that the wounds
Would always leave a scar.
I know that day is near
When I know you will never say what I
longed to hear.
The thread is packed in a roll
It has a long way to go.
But the bundle has an end too,
Save it,
Till it slips.

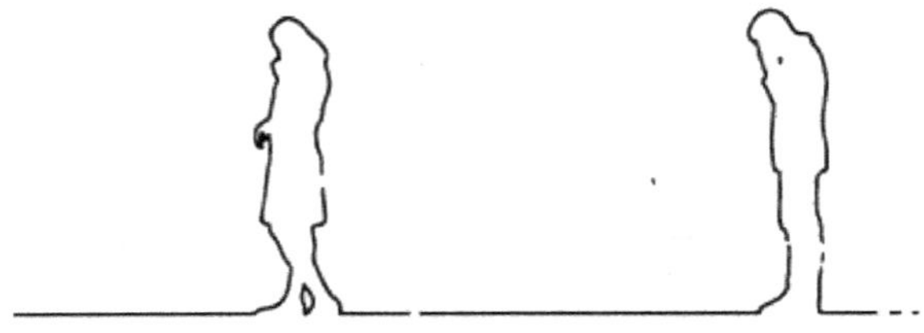

Army of two

Love is a team play.
And I thought we were a team of two,
On the same side of bay,
Fighting every demon that comes in our way.
You get hurt in war.
I pick you, clean you,
And up you roar.
For the times you loved me in the past,
You picked several teams.
Now you have an army.
But you, you are the only one I lived by,
And my reign ends with you.

Sad song

It aches my hurt
And crushes my soul
It drains my blood
To see my love
Sing ballads to me
But not for me
But for his old true love.

Winter fell

My heart just spoke of the blue devils,
The ones which rise after a heartbreak.
It completely forgot how the perennial May
Night Sage blooms,
From the dead, every two years.
Or how fetching a garden of peonies looks
like.
My heart? It beats like a tree in autumn,
The one with branches, after the winter fall.
Until, it fell for you.

Oblivion

In a world full of antagonism and enmity,
Where there is no trace of goodwill,
Lived this fragile soul, refined and radiant.
Puzzled by the people around, the way every
human functioned,
Asked herself, "Why is she different?"
"Why is she not as pious as other women?"
"Why is she so muddled about things around
her?"
"Why is she so... oblivious?"

Anxious, she set out to see the world.
The poverty around, shook her.
Ruthless behavior on animals, shook her.

Two perfect sides of a coin—the rich and
poor—shook her.
She was startled and totally puzzled.
She was completely, oblivious.

Days passed, and she couldn't bear it
anymore,
She strived hard, to bring a "change"
A change, that might restore the goodwill
that was lost.
One person can bring a change, yes
But what could this little soul, suppressed and
overpowered with pessimism do?
Once again, a ray of hope gone in vain.
And goodwill, sank into Oblivion.

Sunflower

How to raise a sunflower, which is so
refreshing to watch?
Fluttering with joy in a field,
Being home to the bees,
Always facing the light,
Beaming with a yellow smile.
Such a warm present of nature.
Petals like rays of sunshine,
Never afraid of the dark.
Completely oblivious to its shadow.
It's a bright euphoria,
Inviting the sweet summer sun.
Loving yourself,
Is like,
A sunflower within you.

The Journey

Three seasons of scars.
It was a gloomy Sunday afternoon.
My empty mind started to unfold the pieces
of past,
Like a cassette on rewind.
Titled 'Scars That Made Me Beautiful' – a series
of three seasons.

Season 1: Bullying.
Metal braces, thick glasses and curly hair were
my personality,
Like a perfect big-sized midget.
Being mocked for 6 hours a day at school,
Who was shy all day and in tears by night.

Season 2: Cheating

This kid was now in her teens,
Bound to toxic love.
Pity, she never played chess because,
She was just a pawn that got played along.

Season 3: The change
I walk with these open wounds to
womanhood.
My scars pulled me down, my heart broke the
vigour,
But my brain was the greatest strength.
It reminded me of the joy to be born,
A chance to live as a kid, a teen, a woman,
Who walks through all phases of life with
conviction.
This series taught me that scars are events
which shape our story,
And what we are told as kids,
Is that every story ends beautifully.

www.ingramcontent.com/pod-product-compliance
Lightning Source LLC
LaVergne TN
LVHW021229200726
843509LV00012B/1458